I Lead Because I Follow...
(What's understood does not have to be explained)

Santiego Rivers

I Lead Because I Follow

(What's Understood Does Not Have to Be Explained)

Copyright © 2021 by Santiego Rivers

All rights reserved. No part of this book may be reproduced or transmitted in any form without the written permission of the author.

ISBN 978-1-7352176-9-7

For years, I struggled with my pride and my fears, so I took a path in life that left me with tears. **(I had to square up)**

For years, I played small when the moment was much too big to give anything but my best. I wanted to fit in with my friends, so I buried my greatness to blend in with the rest.

The hardest thing in life is not when other people do not understand your path or your journey in life. The real dilemma is when you don't realize the path or destination of your life.

Fear stops many people from achieving greatness.

The tipping point in my life came when I realized that the way I was living my life was not working for my well-being. So, I decided to live my life in a way that would bring pleasure to the all-seeing.

I was created to serve… The best of me has always been found in my service to others. The rest of me had to learn to get on board to help me lead my Sistars and Brothers.

Table of Content

All Good Will Be Attacked (5)

The facts about the truth (6)

When I think about a leader (7-8)

When I think about a follower (9-10)

When is it time to lead? (11-12)

Too Many Chiefs and Not Enough Indians (13-14)

Approval rating (15-18)

Having morals and standards (19-20)

It's my passion that drives me (21-22)

When a leader steps into the room (23-24)

What is understood does not have to be explained (25-28)

All "Good" will be attacked

There are times in my life where I stood up, but my mind wanted me to sit back down. Fear makes cowards of us all, but courage gives us the strength to endure.

Silence is a form of agreeance, and I can't entirely agree or choose to remain silent in the presence of wrongdoing.

When you have a mindset like this, you will surely put yourself on the radar of those who don't share your same feelings.

I knew that you would be considered a threat to those who do not share the same feelings as you if you care about what you do.

Those people will twist your words and use their version of the truth to represent the facts improperly.

Standing for what is right or needed will mostly bring you discomfort, ridicule, and pain. **(Colin Kaepernick)**

When you're tempted to quit, remember why you started

The facts about the truth

Truth is defined as that which is valid or in accordance with _fact_ or reality. **Facts** are defined as information used as evidence or as part of a report.

The following should be noted:

"All truth passes through three stages. First, it is ridiculed. Second, it is violently opposed. Third, it is accepted as being **self**-evident."
- **Arthur Schopenhauer**

The truth is, most people who lead are not even qualified to be considered good followers. These people are selfish, egotistical, self-serving, arrogant, untrustworthy & unfit to represent those in need of real leadership.

I am sure that we can write books on the people who fit this category, but I do not believe in giving attention to those types of people.

When I think about a leader

A leader must help make sense of a situation and give it clarity to those around them.

A leader must understand that they lead to serve and not lead to others' control.

In order to be an effective leader, you need to know why you lead. It would be best if you also inspired others to become a better version of themselves to benefit humanity. Leading without a clear purpose is like taking a trip without having a destination.

History is full of people who led for all the wrong reasons but is greatly admired by those who followed because they needed an excuse to express their deepest desires.

1. **Adolf Hitler** (1889-1945)
2. **Joseph Stalin** (1878-1953)
3. **Vlad the Impaler** (1431-1476/77)
4. **Pol Pot** (1925-1998)
5. **Heinrich Himmler** (1900-1945)
6. **Saddam Hussein** (1937-2006)
7. **Idi Amin** (1952-2003)
8. **Ivan the Terrible** (1530-1584)

I never wanted to be a leader. I did not want the responsibility of having other people count on me to make decisions that I felt they could independently.

I knew that the same people who praised you when times were good would grow to hate you when times got a little rough. Times will always be bad/ tough before they get better. This is the natural process. Anything different than that should be considered fool's gold because why would there be a need for a leader to lead if everything is working out fine? The following is how I strongly feel:

To lead is to serve…I stand on this

The fabric/ roots of all good leaders are their ability and willingness to be in the service of others. A good leader is a great follower. In order to lead, you must follow a code/ principal bigger than yourself.

The Code/ principal must be the foundation that stands long after your demise. Therefore, leaders' risk is great because they realize that the reward will be even more significant in the end.

Faith & hard work moves mountains

When I think about a follower

Followers are the backbone of any group, club, or organization. The best leaders started as followers before they made their transition to become a leader.

To be a good leader, you must be an excellent follower/ pupil. It takes humility and the ability to be humble to understand the power of showing mercy instead of strength.

A real leader/king never shows power when there is no threat/or foe present.

A follower who is willing to learn will discover why, how, and when it is time for a leader to step up and lead.

You don't put a child behind the wheels of a vehicle or take them hunting without teaching them the responsibility involved of controlling or having so much power in their hands.

Every action has a reaction that requires thought before acting. Emotions should never be why you act /react because, over time, your feelings will change.

The decisions and choices that you made during your emotions cannot be taken back. Once a ripple is made in the water, the situation must now run its course.

Life is not a videogame; you can restart when you know that you have made a wrong decision. Life becomes the result of our actions or a lack thereof.

As a former boxing and wrestling coach, I refused to train anyone without making sure they knew about the importance of discipline and having the right mindset.

I did not teach my pupils to fight. I taught my pupils the skills to defend themselves when they could not walk away from danger.

It takes more courage to walk away from a fight than to engage in a battle. The skills you learn while under the guidance of a leader become the values and lessons you will teach others when leading others.

When is it time to lead?

The right time to lead is when people need someone to stand up or speak for those who don't have a voice.

The hardest thing to do as a leader is walk away from a situation where your presence or guidance could make a difference in someone else's life.

I remembered as a child I was bullied at school. One day someone took the time to confront the person who was bullying me. That situation had a significant impact on my life.

Most of the fights that I got into after I was protected from my bully as a youth was from me standing up for people who were bullied by others.

By nature, I am a gentle soul, but there were times in my life that introduced myself and others to the darkness that dwelled deep inside me.

The only thing that I fear in life today is me. I know what hides behind my silence and the rage that lives within me.

Until I could come to peace with my dual nature and learn to be slow to anger, I could not lead others.

How can you properly lead others when you cannot control yourself beyond your emotions? The test that we face in life will give you a testimony that you can share with others who need to conquer or face some of the obstacles you learned how to deal with or still overcoming on your self-discovery journey.

Just because you are a leader, it does not mean that you cannot or will not learn anything new. Perfection is the flaw or mistake that the unlearnt makes time and time again.

The situation will dictate when it is the right time to lead. The right time to lead is when you cannot turn away or turn a blind eye to injustice.

When you decide to lead or take a stand; You become driven with a passion that burns inside, inspiring you to accomplish many incredible feats in life.

Too Many Chiefs and Not Enough Indians

Everybody wants to be a leader, except the people who were born to lead. If you took the time to research some of the most outstanding leaders in history, you would discover that they became leaders based upon the need and not the want.

People like Frederick Douglas, Harriet Tubman, Nat Turner, Sojourner Truth, Medgar Evers, Martin Luther King, & Malcolm X lead others because they wanted to help others, not simply because they wanted to become a leader.

When you stand front and center, you make yourself a target to everybody. It will not be just your good qualities that stand-out or the noble act you are doing by taking a stand; people will judge you by the imperfections in your life that are not even perfect in their lives.

(For clarity, let me repeat It)

People will judge you by the imperfections in your life that are not even perfect in their lives. The hate is accurate; the love is what is fake.

Being a leader, you not only make yourself a target to the people who despise you; the people you are trying to help sometimes become your biggest enemies.

If you look at it from a biblical standpoint:

Who betrayed Jesus? Judas Iscariot was one of the original disciples of Jesus Christ. However, when things got tense, he quickly sold out the Son of God for a mere 30 silver coins.

If you look at it from a historical standpoint:

Julius Caesar considered Brutus one of his closest friends, but he was part of the group that assassinated him." Ettu, Brute"?

Your enemy may not always try to take your life. Most times, your enemy takes something more important to you. Your enemy will try to assassinate your name and character as a person.

It is hard to be considered a person of conviction when your name and character are in question.

A good leader is rooted in principle, morals, strong character, faith & hard work. A good leader is **"Not perfect,"** but they are **"Perfect"** in their willingness to serve others despite their limitations and their flaws as a person.

As I mentioned earlier, even Martin Luther King Jr. had people around him who wanted to silence him because they felt that he would make it harder for the people he was trying to help.

The most important thing a leader needs to learn is that you can't help those who do not want help. A lesson that all lifeguards are trained to know is that someone must be willing to help themselves before you can assist them in their survival.

Approval Ratings

Martin Luther King Had a <u>75 Percent Disapproval Rating</u> in the Year of His Death. What do you think the approval rating was for Rosa Park, Medgar Evers, or anyone leading the fight for making a change in America's system?

Even Abraham Lincoln was shunned by the powers that be when he was forced to honor the Emancipation Proclamation. Evidence of him being shunned can be found when you line up all the American coins and see that he is not facing the same way as all the other former Presidents.

This is a highly debated topic, but the facts remain that there is no such thing as power moves and political decisions made by accident.

Life is a game of chess and not checkers

We currently live in a society where truth and acceptance are based on the number of likes or followers.

We forget that the Devil was not cast down to Earth alone. He also had lots of followers who followed him to his banishment from Heaven.

Even Jesus had 12 disciples, but only one of them was present when he died on the cross.

The numbers of like you get does not mean anything when you stand for something in life. Having integrity, true grit & character cannot be sold or bought. These things are earned over time.

It takes conviction to stand for something bigger than yourself. It takes courage to speak out when other people around you remain silent in the presents of injustice/wrongdoing. Your principle must be stronger than your fears of being ridiculed and shunned by your peers.

When it comes to standing alone or not going with the crowd when their beliefs conflict with your integrity, a person will not be popular amongst their peers.

The easiest thing to do in life is sit down instead of taking a stand for a needed cause. I had stood firm even when fear and doubt filled my mind.

I wanted to sit down and remain silent, but I was taught that a coward dies a thousand deaths, so I stood.

I am considered an introvert to those who do not know me because I cannot try and fit where I don't belong. Life has taught me to be in a group; you sometimes must compromise who you are not to make those around you feel uncomfortable about what they are not.

To those who know me, they understand that I say what I mean, and I mean what I say. I don't smile in front of your face and gossip behind your back.

My "Yes" means "Yes' and my "No's" mean "No."

I find it easier to change my company than to change who I am as a person. I discovered it is better to be around people that make you better as a person and remove yourself from the company of those who do not improve your growth as a person. The tough choices that you refuse to make today, life will make it for you eventually.

Having morals and standards

If you have any morals or standards in you, it would be tough to lead or follow someone lacking in either category.

People with morals and standards would relatively stand-alone than try to fit in with others, which makes them question the fiber of their existence.

My life has a purpose, and I know that purpose. **(To serve others)** Anyone who does not share my calling to be in others' service does not warrant my attention when I am fulfilling my calling.

My feeling on this matter does not mean that I do not have associates in my life who do not have the same calling; it simply means that they are not people who I call a friend or someone in my close circle.

When you work a **9 to 5** job, you primarily work with colleagues, not your real friend, most of the time. Some people may call their colleagues at their job work friends, which means that you are friendly with them at work, but they are not people you would generally socialize with outside of work.

Either you or your colleagues lack or display morals and standards, which is why the relationship does not work beyond your job.

Having morals and standards is not something you can turn on and off. Anyone who feels differently should be avoided like the plague. There is no compromising when it comes to having or displaying morals and standards.

Those "*Entitled*" people may want to argue this point, but I will never waste my breath or time arguing with fools. When you argue with fools in public, it becomes hard to determine who is the fool. **(Think about that)**

Having Morals and Standards is one of the critical principles of a great follower and essential quality for a good leader.

It's my passion that drives me

You must love what you do to be effective at it for a long time. It will take faith, hard work, prayer, and patience to sustain you over time.

Caring for the welfare and the Equity of others is what I love to do. It takes a person to be willing to be the reason that someone else feels loved, supported, respected, and appreciated.

I like to think that I have proven to be that type of person throughout my life.

It took me years to accept and make peace with doing what I was called to do. A person can only run from their calling for so long until they run smack into the thing that they were running from.

Running into the thing that I was avoiding was my reality. Facing my reality fueled my passion for pursuing my calling in life.

When you discover what drives you in life, you find out the purpose of your life.

Discovering my purpose in life fueled my passion for making my dreams into reality.

I am not saying that the path that I choose to take in life was easy; I will say that the course that I decided to take was worth it, being in others' service.

I am not mentally a **9 to 5** worker, but I do work at a so-called **9 to 5** job because it allows me the opportunity to work with young adolescents.

A leader is willing to go wherever their service is needed the most. I travel an hour to work each day and deal with adults with more childish behaviors than the young adolescents we try to help.

There must be a need for a leader to lead, and the demand must be greater than the fear to turn and walk away.

When a leader steps into the room

The presence of a "Good" leader changes the atmosphere in the room. Chaos begins to have an order when a leader is present. Followers start to remember why they follow, and leaders show why they lead.

Leaders make the following statements true:

- The success of a team or group depends upon good leadership.
- Leaders demand a higher standard from themselves and others.
- Leaders become the example that they expect from their followers
- Leaders understand you must do what is best for the group and not just the individual

The presence of a good leader is priceless, while a lousy leader's reign can be detrimental to the group.

Good leaders will eventually step back to allow other the opportunity to step up and take on more responsibilities. Leaders teach others how to lead when the time is right for them to lead.

There are many ways that a person can lead, and sometimes you will have to lead-based upon the people you oversee overseeing.

The way that you lead young adults would be different than if you oversaw teaching actual adults.

A good leader can communicate to their crowd, ensuring that the message and the meaning they are delivering are appropriately received.

Leadership is not about titles and receiving praises from others. Leadership is about a person's ability to influence or bring out the best in others while letting the best of you lead by example.

Leaders understand the importance of being the example you want to see in the world and the people around you.

Leaders don't ask anyone to do anything that they would not do themselves. What you do will always outweigh what you say.

What is understood does not have to be explained

Find something positive in your life that you gravitate to and that can keep your attention. It would help if you had something to motivate you when you start to think about quitting. Find the one thing that you would do for free if you had the opportunity to do it.

For me, it was working with young adults and encouraging adults to become the best version of themselves. I have done this as a volunteer and now as a paid Behavior Specialist.

Caring for the welfare and the Equity of others does not make you weak. Learning to put others first is a quality that makes you unique.

When you put meaning behind your passion, it will take you in a life direction meant for you to travel. What will you discover when the rubber hits the road and you now have a purpose in your life?

You will first become a dedicated student to learning the skills/lessons it will take to achieve your goals. You will then begin to take your journey inwards to remove/change anything that will prevent you from becoming the best version of yourself.

You will have to change who you are to become the person you want to become. If the old version of you were working for your best interest, then you would already have everything that you desire from life.

These are some of the lessons that the student/follower must learn before becoming a good leader. To become a good leader, you must be an excellent follower.

The road is hard, but the journey is worth it once you have finally reached your destination. There is greatness within you that is ready to be unleashed.

The greatness inside of you is meant for you to share with the world. Your greatness is the gift that is intended to be shared with others.

Stop looking for or depending on the approval of others. You don't need someone else to say "Attaboy" to motivate you to keep trying.

No one else is supposed to understand or undervalue your gift because it is not theirs to share. Your gift/talent was given to you so that you can share it with the world.

The only thing you must do is to be willing to walk by faith until you can see the fruits of your labor come to pass. The only certainty in life is change. Will you make the change in your life that inspires others who have watched your journey to success?

Don't say yes with words and let your actions let you down. Make a stand and become the person you want to be.

References

- *essay-why-martin-luther-king-had-75-percent-disapproval-rating-year-his-death*. (n.d.). History. GA. Edu. Retrieved March 29, 2021, from https://history.uga.edu/

- *viralnova.com*. (n.d.). Viralnova.Com. Retrieved March 29, 2021, from https://viralnova.com/famous-betrayals/

www.ingramcontent.com/pod-product-compliance
Lightning Source LLC
Chambersburg PA
CBHW071014160426
43193CB00012B/2048